FAST
PRAY
SHARE

RAMADAN REFLECTIONS

D1361628

TUGHRA BOOKS

FAST

PRAY

SHARE

RAMADAN REFLECTIONS

Lawrence Brazier - Abdul Basit Jamal Bukhari - M. Fethullah Gülen
Sana Khan - Cassandra Lawrence - Hannah Matus - Martha Trunk
Rabbi Burton Visotzky - Jeff Wearden - Hakan Yesilova

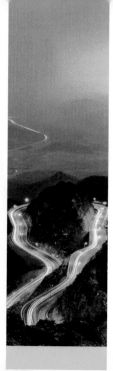

CONTENTS

INTRODUCTION

Celebrated by almost 2 billion Muslims around the world, Ramadan is a month filled with prayer, fasting, and charity. As many Muslims withdraw from the worldly affairs into Ramadan's spiritual retreat, they break bread together with family and neighbors after a daylong fast from dawn to sunset. It is a time devoted to overcoming our weaknesses and discovering our inner potentials.

Fasting is an ancient form of worship practiced in many faith traditions. Thus, in diverse societies, Muslims are joined by friends and colleagues from other traditions during Ramadan to reinforce community spirit and honor this practice with gratitude.

Featuring authors from different faith traditions *Fast-Pray-Eat-Share: Ramadan Reflections* aims to contribute to the rejuvenating spirit of this holy month.

THE "BORDERLINE"

BETWEEN COMMON SENSE AND DESIRE

by Lawrence Brazier

It may be reasonable to suggest that the ways of God—for the most part mysterious—sometimes include a portion of logic. After all, we are informed that God loves His children and would have them be healthy and content. I read from a mystic source about a man being asked if he loved humanity. "I do, indeed," he said. "Then why," asked the mystic, "do you treat yourself so badly?"

If we equate the material forces we are subjected to as toxic (the fast of Ramadan is not merely a physical detox, but also a detox of the soul), then one may suggest that the prophets went cold turkey on the world. The fast of Ramadan is, however, nowhere near as extreme. One is required to pull back a little, exercise restraint, and get perspective.

In the meantime, some of the positive media resources at our disposal have made clear to most non-Muslims the true meaning of jihad, which is working through one's own inner struggles. Quite obviously our inner world will be sharply accentuated during a period of fasting. Contrary to common conduct, we are informed that whatever problems one is confronted with, whether personal relationships or even financial difficulties, they should be faced by fasting. In our complex world, the opposite is generally undertaken. When a crisis arises, the usual attitude is to blot out a feeling of desperation with excess, the use of alcohol, drugs, and all manner of consumption. But sometimes, the most effective recourse is to simply lay aside for a while the burdens of what we often call necessity. If we are to see most of our so-called "needs" as perhaps simply add-ons to our lives, then we might be able to "get real," as my American colleagues might say. To meet the challenge and provide for our worldly needs is not to be denied, but perspective and a sensitive awareness of the material claims made by our hearts and minds would be useful. It is here that the fast of Ramadan becomes vital—and often revealing.

I suppose I could explain that as a non-Muslim journalist undertaking the fast of Ramadan has always been a matter of research. But not so. I have many Muslim friends, and I always felt that it was something I should do. Moreover, I had a deep wish to experience the mystic aspects of which I had been informed.

The five pillars of Islam are a profession of faith—the affirmation that there is no god but God and that Muhammad is His Messenger—prayer, the giving of alms, pilgrimage to Mecca, and fasting.

Focus is the keyword, and good intention. The laid down periods of fasting help us to do what we know, in all honesty, is right for us. And at the same time that means benefitting the people around us, our families, neighbors, the community at large.

It would be wrong to suggest that the outer and inner fast is easy. No food, water, alcohol, or nicotine during the hours of daylight are the basic requirements. The inner fast means subjugation of bad thinking, arguing, philosophizing, and sex.

The first couple of days are obviously the most difficult. At around twelve noon the pangs of hunger are insistent. Devout Muslims spend such times in prayer. The evening comes and, at the proscribed moment—when daylight is gone, when some say that the difference between a black and white cotton is not discernible—it is time to eat. Experts in bodily functions and the experienced know that relief, which generally means freedom from the demands of the body, comes after about three days. It is a physical fact. Nevertheless, it is best not to forget that God is behind everything.

PERIODS OF FASTING HELP US TO DO WHAT WE KNOW IS RIGHT FOR US.

Many years ago, I enjoyed a daydream about equanimity, which for me meant a quiet mind. I read of the mystic who said that he was walking around, feeling quite happy, *with nothing much on his mind*. What a wonderful condition that must be. I do not believe we can learn to be good, but we may have a chance of unlearning how to be bad. In my daydream I pictured a desert *riad*, the sublime architecture of which stuns the mind. There will naturally be the prerequisite inner courtyard. There will be a colonnaded walk around the divine fountain, which gurgles ever so discretely. I am wearing a robe and soft slippers. I walk sedately among the columns, murmuring a few verses from something or other, perhaps even from the Quran. It would be the time for finer feelings to emerge, and for passions to diminish, as I slowly lose myself.

In the everyday world, of course, the vast majority of Muslims do not possess a *riad*, and they do not have the energy to murmur anything at all beyond a fervent wish for the clock to show a different face. Those poorer multitudes are out there, doing their best to survive the onslaught of a secular existence that is insistently temporal. It is said that by four in the afternoon, the cigarette smokers are going out of the minds. What in Arabic is called the *nafs* can be comfortably translated into English as lower forces, but in the ways of the world, with appetites attached. Ramadan has sometimes allowed me to fairly easily discern the "borderline" between common sense and desire. You need to be alert, though! A slip in awareness can have you slathering into a cream cake in no time.

We are also much too active in the world. An invitation to visit a daughter means that she will cook for us and one can hardly refuse. We eat and drink. I am to eventually count four alcoholic drinks during this month.

"RAMADAN ALTERED MY MIND. I BEGAN TO CARE ABOUT DIFFERENT ASPECTS OF LIFE. MY FEELINGS ABOUT PEOPLE IN NEED BECAME ACUTE."

The mystic, again: "You can do anything you like in this world as long as you don't hurt anybody." Thoughts arising in this way are also a blessing because one is not thinking anything of a bloodcurdling nature. God is thus, good.

Ramadan, in my experience, seems to go okay after the first unaccustomed onslaught of hunger. I was also surprised to find another "me" inside, and I lost a couple of kilograms. It is common knowledge that a one-liter carton of milk weighs one kilogram. Thus, the loss of ten kilograms of body weight can be viewed as not dragging ten cartons of milk around with you. I have read extreme stories of people losing 15 or even 20 cartons.

Ramadan altered my mind (honestly). I began to care about different aspects of life. My feelings about people in need became acute. I also began to consider what senseless commodities are purchased by consumers. There is a lovely quote from Shaker philosophy: "Don't make anything unless it is necessary and useful; but if it is both necessary and useful don't hesitate to make it beautiful."

We were driving through a small town, and a large man strolled casually, obliquely across the road in front of our car. His insouciance was insulting. Anger flared within me. I slowed but gunned the engine as we passed him. If there were minus points to be acquired I had acquired the maximum.

Visitors arrived. I "borrowed" one cigarette, ate one small thing on a cocktail stick, drank half a glass of water and one small cup of black tea. The visitors fortunately refused wine. I was convinced that hospitality should be shown so that guests were not embarrassed or felt unwanted.

When one puts one's appetites (the naughty Arabic *nafs*) on hold, they sulk. Confusion is the result, and one's own small blobs of chaos will be added to an already chaotic world. Ramadan is about personal responsibility, not sinning inwardly, not romping into a philosophical debate. I felt the nafs having a field day. I really must get quiet, but it is so very difficult for a writer to acquire grace, but isn't that always the case? God is not only great; He is the origin of all wisdom.

Finally, Eid al-Fitr—the celebration ceremony marking the end of Ramadan—arrives. I had somehow floated through the last ten days of the month of fasting. For a brief period, I experienced what Christians call "the peace that passeth all understanding." This experience and other experiences, according to the lights of the recipient, come during the so-called "night(s) of power," when God's grace is poured down. These are the blessings that make Ramadan such an inspiring endeavor.

Inner worship is a prayer that prays of itself. Something inside a person, the soul, begins to pray.

THE REAL PURPOSE OF FASTING

by Abdul Basit Jamal Bukhari

When one hears the word Ramadan, thoughts of eating tasty food at iftar (breaking of the fast) comes to one's mind. The holy month culminates at a grand feasting during Eid. For children, *iftar* and *Eid* are the most exciting time of the calendar. Some people never grow out of this understanding of Ramadan, even as they age. Is this what the month of fasting is about? Surely not, because in the early days of Islam, Prophet Muhammad (pbuh) and his companions at times had nothing to eat, let alone for a feast.

There is something God wants cooked in us

Fasting is not the end in itself; rather, God prescribed fasting as a tool for achieving something very important: taqwa.

> *"O you who have believed, decreed upon you is fasting as it was decreed upon those before you, so that you may become of those having taqwa."* (Quran 2:183)

Taqwa simply means to be conscious of God in your thinking. To seek His refuge from being someone who does not love Him. Thus, taqwa motivates a person to perform righteous deeds and avoid forbidden activities.

***Taqwa* is a way of thinking**

A story in the Quran informs us about Habil and Qabil (without giving their names), the two sons of Adam (pbuh). The story tells that even though both had sacrificed something for God, God only accepted the sacrifice of Habil and rejected the sacrifice of Qabil.

Taif, Saudi Arabia

"IF YOU RAISE YOUR HAND TO KILL ME, I WILL NOT RAISE MINE TO KILL YOU, BECAUSE I FEAR GOD—THE LORD OF ALL THE WORLDS."

QURAN 5:28

"God only accepts the sacrifice of those who have taqwa" (Quran 5:27).

Habil possessed taqwa and this is what made him different from Qabil. Habil was conscious of God, that He wants us to do better, and become deserving of paradise, and that Satan wants each child of Adam (pbuh) to be deserving of hell. So, when Qabil came to kill his stronger brother, Habil said, *"If you raise your hand to kill me, I will not raise mine to kill you, because I fear God—the Lord of all the worlds"* (Quran 5:28). Before dying, Habil used the technique of reverse psychology and tried to stop his brother by giving him awareness that he was committing a grave sin. Habil did not try to kill him; he did not attack back. Habil died giving his brother an opportunity to repent, and as we learn in the Quran, Qabil actually did repent. Had Habil killed Qabil even as an act of self-defense, Qabil's book of deeds would have closed with him trying to kill a chosen man of God. Habil did what he did because his thinking had taqwa. Peace be upon Habil.

As a child of Adam, Prophet Muhammad (pbuh) spoke like Habil to the other children of Adam, who tried to stone him to death in Taif. After he barely made it out of town, the angel Jibreel (Gabriel) (pbuh) came to him and informed him that God had sent him to seek his permission to destroy the city where the Prophet was stoned. Jibreel (pbuh) was informing the Prophet that just like Habil, he was stronger than people of Taif. May peace be upon the great prophet; he asked Jibreel to go back, saying he hopes that the people of Taif might change in the future and become deserving of paradise. Just as Qabil, the people of Taif did repent later on. Prophet Muhammad (pbuh) did what he did because he had taqwa. Not everyone may be able to rise to such a degree of taqwa, but at least they can begin with something smaller, something like, "even if you abuse me, I won't abuse you" or "even if you desire ill for me, I will not desire ill for you."

So, when God said, *"O you who have believed, decreed upon you is fasting as it was*

16

decreed upon those before you, so that you may become of those having taqwa," the Prophet (pbuh) who knew best what God meant, taught his followers not to retaliate, saying, *"Don't behave foolishly or imprudently while fasting, if somebody attacks you or abuses you, say I am fasting"* (Bukhari book 31 hadith 118 & 128). The Prophet (pbuh) was teaching one of the most evident signs of *taqwa*: that you don't return abuse or hurt that others cause you. One who retaliates acts foolishly, and fools play into the hands of Satan, unaware that he causes conflict, hatred, and enmity, while God wants harmony, love, and friendship. Surely the fools run away from a single drop of alcohol and call the gamblers sinners, but eagerly drink hatred and engage in enmity: *"Satan's plan is to stir up enmity and hatred between you with alcohol and gambling"* (Quran 5:91). Surely fools are worse in the scheme of things.

"THEN GOD SENT FORTH A RAVEN, SCRATCHING IN THE EARTH, TO SHOW HIM HOW HE MIGHT COVER THE CORPSE OF HIS BROTHER"

QURAN 5:31

Satan calls you to be fools, while fasting calls you to be a great one by urging you to overcome your lower self. Surely the lower self doesn't want to keep the mouth shut; it wants to eat and not fast, just like it wants to return the abuses and not remain silent. God wants you to defeat your lower self and say to it, "No! I will not eat nor drink even if you desire it," so that you may be trained to say "No" to your lower self and in the matter of egoistic behaviour you may be able to say, "No! I will not return the abuses or retaliate."

O children of Adam! It's a holy month that calls you to a holy act so that you may become holy men and women. So, this Ramadan, make sure you win the battle against your carnal soul (*jihad al-nafs*) and build a personality that has taqwa.

Jama Masjid
New Delhi, India

Indeed, taqwa alone is the criterion of greatness in the sight of God. God says in the Quran, "*O mankind! We have created you from a male and a female, and made you into nations and tribes, that you may know one another. Verily, the most honorable of you with God is the one who has taqwa. Verily, God is All-Knowing, All-Aware*" (49:13).

Great people who develop taqwa are gifted with the precious gift of finding guidance in the great Quran: "*This is the book about which there is no doubt, a guidance for those with taqwa*" (2:2). This guidance from the Quran is what each believer needs to have in this life.

ABDUL BASIT JAMAL BUKHARI is a writer and researcher in Islamic studies. He is based in New Delhi.

RAMADAN

THE SUM OF SPIRITUAL JOYS

by M. Fethullah Gülen

No month of the year can sail along with as much joy that never fades and everlasting pleasure and love, as the month of Ramadan. Presenting the spirit, essence, and true meaning of all the gentle seasons of the year, the days and nights of Ramadan embrace hearts with their exclusive bliss, charm, and love, exciting them with an enthusiasm for life.

The days of Ramadan all over the world are the sum of our spiritual joys, the helix of the divine light of progress, and the sphere of opportunity for the growth of all human virtues.

Communicating a special aura to the hearts, Ramadan reunites those parts of society that have fallen out of touch with one another; opening the way for all those in solitude to congregate, eliminating feelings of longing away from home. It is a banquet of emotions and ideas for everyone in varying dimensions, and awakes us all, one more time, to life.

Ramadan, above all, is the month of the Qur'an; in this regard even the ones who have distanced themselves from the Qur'an throughout the year, those who are parched with a burning thirst, find themselves in this radiating ambience. These days replenish the valleys of the psyches which have almost dried out with the spirit, meaning and mystery of the Qur'an; it transforms the heart into a flower garden

Selimiye Mosque
Edirne, Türkiye

and elates these people with the joy of existence. Then, they sense and receive the entire cosmos by and through the Qur'an, appreciating that the whole creation process is manifested therein, and are meek in astonishment and reverence. Sometimes they breathe with tears, and with tears do they discharge what they keep inside. They feel the veils have been removed, and they are now closer to God and in an abundance of joy.

The divine contents of the Qur'an can be comprehended only by those who can both hear the sound of the entire cosmos, and are also attuned to the human soul's melody, a melody composed of fear and hope, worry and joy, dolor and cheer, all at the same time. The timeless souls who can listen to the Qur'an as if it has been sent just for them can experience the flavor of paradisical fruits, the colors and beauty and the panoramic falls of the gardens and bays of the Heaven, and become enthusiastic and energized. In the life philosophy of these people, metaphysics completes physics; meaning becomes the true content and gist of the matter, and everything becomes visible with their true value. An imaginary mystery is sensed on the countenances of these people, as if a secret intuition has been inspired by their receptiveness to the infinite sphere of the Divine Names and Attributes; a maturity, a satisfaction, a purity, a sincerity imbued by the piety of days fully engaged with the Qur'an. In no month

THE DIVINE CONTENTS OF THE QUR'AN CAN BE COMPREHENDED ONLY BY THOSE WHO CAN BOTH HEAR THE SOUND OF THE ENTIRE COSMOS, AND ARE ALSO ATTUNED TO THE HUMAN SOUL'S MELODY, A MELODY COMPOSED OF FEAR AND HOPE, WORRY AND JOY, DOLOR AND CHEER, ALL AT THE SAME TIME.

other than the "Qur'an-oriented" Ramadan are the nights and days differentiated by different illuminations. Indeed, during Ramadan, the originality of the Qur'an shines in every glowing face.

Every single soul becomes purified from all spiritual shortcomings in an unprecedented dimension in Ramadan. This month grants such an abundance and prolificacy that almost everyone that shelters in its shadow can benefit from its wealth and riches and attain a spiritual sultanate.

During the whole of Ramadan, the nights enfold everything in their mysteries – mysteries so intimate and amiable – the days which embrace one's emotions and thoughts with an unaccustomed pleasure are so warm and soft, the faces in faith are so affectionate and informed, the sounds that summon one to God are so caring, and above all, the total meaning of these are so touching that the ones who can open their hearts to this month of mercy, even temporarily, welcome the happiness of heaven after they have unburdened themselves of their worries and sorrows, one by one.

M. FETHULLAH GÜLEN is an Islamic scholar and author of *The Messenger of God: Muhammad.*

KEY TO THE WORLD'S

GREATEST TREASURE

by Sana Khan

Consider this scenario.

A 60-year-old Muslim patient with diabetes makes an appointment with his physician to come up with a plan for adjustment to his usual insulin dose for the next month.

"I won't be eating anything in the hours between dawn and dusk for the next thirty days," he explains.

The physician reluctantly admits that it is possible, but proceeds to probe the necessity of such a change, especially for the whole thirty days.

"Of course, the best thing is to leave the dose as is," the physician says, switching to a practiced authoritative tone reserved for such moments. "Your blood sugars are doing great. Perhaps consider taking every other day off."

The well-meaning physician is certain that a few more such statements will steer the conversation away from making any significant changes to the patient's insulin regimen. But, to the physician's surprise, the patient politely refuses the compromise, stating that he wants to give it his best shot, and if a true medical reason were to come up over the course of the month, he will revisit the physician's suggestion. [1]

As a practicing physician, I can tell you that in the months leading up to Ramadan, such a scenario is anything but uncommon. My non-Muslim colleagues are often perplexed after these patient encounters, wondering why Muslims are so adamant about observing the Ramadan fast, which requires them to abstain from any food and water from sunrise to sunset—a period of over twelve hours in most states across the United States.

In all honesty, even as a Muslim physician, I have found it difficult to answer this question in a way that truly encompasses the spiritual and emotional reasons behind why so many Muslims cannot fathom letting go of a Ramadan fast, even those who may otherwise struggle with the basic obligation of observing the five daily prayers (May God forgive us all, ameen).

As is the promise of God, when we sincerely seek, He uncovers for us the answer, often in a way that leaves us wondering how we never perceived it before. The secret of Muslims' collective devotion to Ramadan

Largely unbeknownst even to them, Muslims naturally begin tapping into this secret source of tranquility as soon as the Ramadan moon is sighted.

permeates innumerable verses in the Qur'an, makes up the foundation of frequently cited Ahadith (traditions of Prophet Muhammad, peace be upon him), and comprises the subject matter of many famous works by the great scholars of Islam.

It is a collective devotion tethered to the feelings of peace and tranquility so many Muslims enjoy in the month of Ramadan, feelings borne out of a source that somehow becomes elusive outside of this month, and feelings that become the reason for the reluctance of Muslims everywhere to miss even a single fast.

Largely unbeknownst even to them, Muslims naturally begin tapping into this secret source of tranquility as soon as the Ramadan moon is sighted. In a flurry of excitement and newfound motivation, members of the family wash themselves for *wudhu*, gather the young and old alike, and drive to the masjid, ready to stand for the first *taraweeh* prayer with the community. Suddenly, gone are the excuses of just one night ago, when staying out to pray in the masjid past midnight seemed like a near impossibility.

And what's more, this despite being fully aware that in only a few hours, a morning meal will need to be consumed while it's still pitch-dark outside. Those, like myself, who aren't used to eating anything until mid-morning, simply ignore the otherwise rock-solid inclinations and sit down for the only meal until evening.

No matter what the day's schedule looks like, Muslims make their best efforts to perform the obligatory daily prayers at a higher level than outside of Ramadan, both in the quality of the prayers, and in the extra consideration for their prescribed times. With no meals to prepare or share, their attention automatically diverts towards other things to fill up the hours, gravitating to that scholarly lecture series a family member recommended. The scholar's words in turn inspire recitation and reflection of the Qur'an, replacing mindless internet surfing or watching the news.

Despite a lack of sleep, food, and drink, Muslims the world over experience a sense of fullness beginning to take place that is hard to explain. It is situated above the gut and the private parts, in the center of the chest, and it is far more satiating than the fulfillment of carnal desires could ever be. This addictive tranquility of the heart is so deeply felt in the month of Ramadan that fasting believers gladly give up the comforts of a consistent schedule, undisturbed sleep, and instant gratification of bodily impulses, in exchange for humanity's most sought-after treasure that no amount of money can buy.

What then, is the key to this treasure of tranquility, and why is it accessible only in the month of Ramadan?

For those whose hearts are ready, the answer is as simple as it gets. It is in the shunning of the inclinations of the self, battling base desires for sleep and hunger, increasing the threshold for discomfort in performing acts of worship that are pleasing to God, that Muslims discover the only currency with which tranquility can be purchased: complete obedience to the command of God, in the way most pleasing to Him.

Allah says in the Qur'an:

"O believers! Enter into Islam wholeheartedly and do not follow Satan's footsteps. Surely, he is your enemy" (2:208)

Scholars of Tafsir have explained this verse to mean that as slaves of God, the submission required from Muslims is one that is complete, independent of reason, logic, convenience and preferences of the self, all of which can be deceptions of Satan. In the month of Ramadan, when the apparent logic against staying up late into the nights is pushed aside, preferences for eating at specific times of day are disregarded, reasons for delaying obligatory prayers in the face of a full work schedule are challenged, all for the pleasure of God alone, the key to the ultimate treasure every human being yearns for is granted to the believer.

Is this to say then that the secret of tranquility lies in the subduing of the human intellect, in conquering our ability to reason, in vanquishing our natural instincts of reflecting on the wisdom in the commands of God?

Absolutely not. It does not befit the infinitely merciful God to first bestow upon humanity the very thing that sets us apart from animals, the intellect, and then reward us for repressing its natural inclinations to think, question, and reflect. In the Qur'an, Allah (swt) Himself says:

No soul can believe except by Allah's will, and He places a blight on those who do not use their intellect" (10:100).

Using the intellect therefore is in itself a command of the One Who created it, a means for us to strengthen our faith by understanding the many benefits for us in the required acts of worship. For instance, the scientific community has only just begun to scratch the surface of the health benefits of fasting, benefits that wouldn't have become apparent without using the God-given powers of the intellect, and benefits that undoubtedly deepen our commitment to fasting regularly.

IT DOES NOT BEFIT THE MERCIFUL GOD TO FIRST BESTOW UPON HUMANITY THE INTELLECT, AND THEN REWARD US FOR REPRESSING ITS NATURAL INCLINATIONS TO THINK, QUESTION, AND REFLECT.

Eyup Sultan Mosque
Istanbul, Türkiye

This is indeed from the Mercy of the Master, that He has not imposed His laws on humanity, but rather illuminated the path to faith through the intellect. What must be recognized by the slave, however, is that the intellect itself is a creation of God, and can never surpass the perfect wisdom of the Creator Himself. With this framework, the believer escapes the predicament of conditional faith: present when the intellect agrees with revelation, absent when a clash occurs.

This is the precise position in which fasting Muslims find themselves in Ramadan when they are commanded to adopt a new, much different, daily schedule than what satisfies their own preferences and logic. It is here, at the limits of reason, that Muslims choose divine revelation over their own intellect; instead of questioning the timing of the Ramadan meals, or arguing the inconvenience of the nightly prayers, or reasoning their way out of performing the obligatory prayers whilst enduring hunger, thirst, and lack of sleep, they make the choice to submit, wholeheartedly, to the commands of God.

In return for giving up the need to satisfy the intellect at the expense of the unlimited wisdom of revelation, God hands fasting Muslims the key to unconditional tranquility, peace, and contentment of the heart.

The real question then becomes: which of us will let go of this key when the month of Ramadan ends, and which of us will guard it beyond the thirty days, striving to live up to the title of the muslim—one who surrenders to God?

The choice is open to all of us.

Note

1. This scenario does not include the patient with uncontrolled or complicated diabetes who is advised against fasting by a physician for true medical reasons. According to Qur'an and Sunnah, such a person is exempt from fasting, as Allah only wants ease, not hardship, for us.

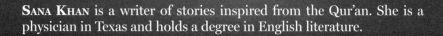

SANA KHAN is a writer of stories inspired from the Qur'an. She is a physician in Texas and holds a degree in English literature.

BECOMING PRESENT TO GOD AND COMMUNITY

by Cassandra Lawrence

For too long in my spiritual imagination, I approached fasting with apprehension, not sure if or how it would bring me closer to the experience of God's love. While fasting is a Christian spiritual practice, it was not part of my immediate community's practice. It has been my friendships with Muslims and Jews that have transformed my own understanding of fasting and what it means to become present to God. My Jewish and Muslim friends have shown me how fasting is a time set apart from our daily lives, that invites and cultivates focus and presence leading to greater clarity on the will of God for us personally and also for the community. I've also learned how fasting is not necessarily a time of depression, guilt, and self-flagellation; rather, it is suffused and grounded in joy. Fasting and Ramadan have been transformed in my imagination to a time set apart that deeply (re)connects all of us, greeting us with joy.

Isaiah 58 opens with shouting that the people are in rebellion. The people are going to the Temple, fasting, seeking forgiveness, and praying to God for favorable judgements, but their actions are not bearing fruit, they are not restoring community. Isaiah says this is not the fast that God wants. God wants us to choose the fast that loosens the bonds of injustice.

It's easy to read this passage and think Isaiah is advocating that we stop fasting and praying, to instead seek justice and mercy with the marginalized and oppressed. This interpretation puts fasting in competition with restoration of community and cutting ourselves off from a transformative process that draws us closer to God. Fasting in this passage is just one part of a process seeking forgiveness for the harms we've committed. Fasting here is not about self-control or even simply avoiding food and water. This fast is a time set apart from daily life for reflection on the word of God, on ourselves, and on community. When I speak to friends who do fast, they talk about how it helps them become present and brings clarity on their life, community, and God. It's in the same family as meditation and deep breathing. It helps us reset. Fasting, linked with prayer, helps us become present to all that is happening around us including where we

have done harm, both individually and communally.

Fasting, in this passage, is a key practice in the process of repentance. Unfortunately, I have often had an overly punishing definition of repentance. The simple definition of repentance means to turn away from the behaviors and beliefs that do harm, and to turn towards the behaviors and beliefs that do good, that bring you closer to God, to healing, and to community. In the process you are making yourself more present and opening yourself to greater clarity from God so that you can know how to love your neighbor.

In nearly every community there is a process of repentance and repair, a process to bring people back into good relationships after they have done harm. If we didn't have this process, we would have surely annihilated ourselves millennia ago. Last fall, I attended my first Yom Kippur service with a friend. This is a day in the Jewish community when

"MY JEWISH AND MUSLIM SIBLINGS BROUGHT THE TEACHINGS OF SCRIPTURE TO LIFE SO THAT I COULD SEE REPENTANCE AND FASTING AS ULTIMATELY AN ACT OF LOVE BRINGING UNCEASING JOY AND THE GRACE OF GOD."

you enter a time of deep reflection on the promises you made to God, and to each other. You reflect on all the ways you fell short of fulfilling those promises, all the ways you did harm, both intentionally and not. You bring these shortcomings and failures to God and community, to seek forgiveness and to turn towards a renewed commitment to follow all God's ways of justice and compassion.

However, the people mentioned in Isaiah, are participating in this practice with their own self-interest in mind. They are using these public displays of repentance to pick fights with each other, and, worse, they continue to treat their family and workers with the same disdain and injustice for which they have supposedly sought forgiveness. They have fasted but have not become present

to the community or to God. In a process meant to bring you face to face with your wrongdoing, they have become blinded by their own self-interest and can no longer see how they are causing harm or acknowledge their responsibility to alleviate the harm of others. This scripture is a message to the times in our lives when we must seek forgiveness, when we must be honest about our failings and the ways we've harmed people.

Becoming present to the community and following a process towards repentance and repair seems like a basic social norm. Yet, in verse 8, Isaiah is saying that not only is God wanting us to care for the poor, the hungry, and the oppressed, but that when we dare to turn towards the work of loosening the bonds of injustice, we dare to move through our guilt and shame towards deeper knowledge and action. For it is then that we find the light of God shining through us like the dawn, like a lamp on the hill. It is then that we, ourselves, are healed. It is then that we become more aware of how others are experiencing the world and how our actions can contribute to others' wellbeing or not. We become aware that this isn't just about me and my shortcomings; it is about our shortcomings as a society. These individual practices build

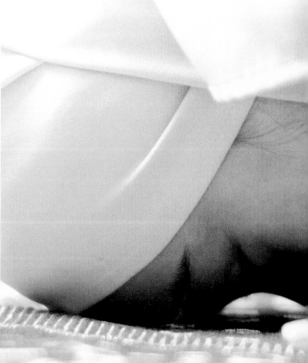

our capacity to look on ourselves and others with compassion. We become aware of all the ways we can grow, be transformed, and move closer to justice and to God. In this process we are met by the grace, mercy, and love of God who wants reconciliation and flourishing for all humanity. It is this that delights God. It is when we become present to and are transformed by this delight that joy abounds and that healing and justice flow down like an ever-flowing stream.

When I attended that Yom Kippur service, I was struck with the joy that suffused the Kol Nidre. When I attend iftars during Ramadan, I see similar joy. Of course, the New Testament has many examples of Jesus and others fasting for some of these same reasons, but for me, seeing how communities use this practice in a variety of ways has transformed me and my practice of prayer. While fasting, prayer, repentance, and repair constitute a serious process, my Jewish and Muslim siblings brought the teachings of scripture to life so that I could see repentance and fasting as ultimately an act of love bringing unceasing joy and the grace of God.

CASSANDRA LAWRENCE is Communications and Community Engagement Manager with the **Shoulder to Shoulder Campaign**, a multifaith coalition-based campaign to connect, equip, and mobilize faith communities and people of goodwill to counter anti-Muslim discrimination in the U.S.

RAMADAN
AT A GLANCE

1. Ramadan is the ninth month of the Islamic lunar calendar.

2. The Qur'anic revelation started first in Ramadan.

3. Fasting in Ramadan is one of the five pillars of Islam (others are testimony of faith, daily prayers, charity, pilgrimage)

4. Fasting starts at dawn and ends at sunset.

5 A pre-dawn meal (suhoor) is recommended and believed to be virtuous.

6. One should not put off breaking the fast (iftar).

7. Eating with family, inviting guests, and especially feeding the poor are strongly advised.

8. One must take precautions against eating too much when breaking the fast (iftar)

9. Fasting does not mean just staying hungry, but also keeping desires and actions under control.

10. Tarawih is a special prayer that is only observed during Ramadan.

11 Ramadan is not only for fasting, but also for prayer, reflection, and studying the Qur'an.

12. A three-day festival (eid al-fitr) is celebrated at the end of Ramadan.

"You will not enter paradise until you believe, and you will not believe until you love one another."

Prophet Muhammad

PEACE BE UPON HIM

WHERE ARE YOU GOING?
WHERE HAVE YOU BEEN?

by Hannah Matus

It's the first day of Ramadan, and Mama is listening to a lecture, as is her wont during these long, hungry days. The speaker laments that someone in his community has passed away, and thus will not have another Ramadan in their life.

Mama looks at you meaningfully. "Heard that?" she asks, as you cut up some onions for the iftar meal.

"Yes, Mama," you murmur. "Very sad." You've heard that type of lecture a dozen times before. The topic leaves your mind, wandering to other things. You hum a popular tune from the radio before you remind yourself that you swore off music for Ramadan.

Later that evening, Baba asks if you want to go to the masjid. You pause before answering, thinking of the early morning of college classes you have the next day. But you think about how it is the first night of Ramadan, and all the interesting people you're bound to see while there.

"Okay, Baba," you say. He warns you that he might be staying late to speak to friends afterwards, so you agree to take separate cars.

You agonize over whether or not to wear makeup before putting on your hijab. You decide to forego any ornamental makeup, but apply a layer of foundation to even out your skin tone. You smile at your virtuous appearance, your radiant flawless face wrapped in a glitzy black hijab.

Your eleven-year-old brother hears you open the front door and demands to be taken along.

"I can't stay waiting for you, Khalid," you say. He scowls at you.

Your mother overhears from her spot on the couch where she grasps her supplication beads and watches Ramadan prayers streamed from Mecca.

"Take him with you," she orders without looking up. "He *wants* to go to the *masjid*." You sigh and walk out the door without a word, leaving it open so he can follow.

He turns on the radio as you drive. You lift up your hand to turn it off, opening your mouth to remind him that he should try not to listen to music in Ramadan, but something stops you. He's been so... brooding lately. You don't want to alienate him. You keep silent as some pop star sings about partying all night in the background. You try not to notice the disparity between the song and where you're headed. You frown at the road ahead, wanting a distraction from your troublesome thoughts, brothers growing up too fast, sisters not knowing where the line of responsibility begins and ends. Your phone pings an incoming text message. You look down.

Going to the masjid? Sarah has texted you. You stretch your thumb wide to send a 👍 one handed. Khalid notices.

"Stop texting and driving!" he shouts.

"Alright, alright, backseat driver," you retort with a smile.

"You don't care about my life or what?" he snaps back, and you can't tell if he's serious or just joking. You drive on in silence.

You pray next to Sarah, who fills you in on all of the insidious gossip during the intervals between prayers.

YOU LOOK UP INTO THE BEAUTIFUL,
CLOUDLESS SKY AND CATCH YOUR BREATH
AT THE AWE OF THE FLORAL MEADOW
BEFORE YOU.

A few weeks later, and the routine of your Ramadan day hasn't changed overly much, except Sarah has stopped going to the masjid. You war with yourself when Baba asks if you will attend.

"I have an exam tomorrow," you say, "so I really need to study." He nods his head and wishes you well with your studying.

You remain at the table and try not to feel guilty for not attending, and for your half-truth. You do have an exam tomorrow, but your professor gave everyone a review sheet of all that will be covered and you've memorized the entire sheet. However, you've just showered and you don't want to put on your hijab and end up with the dreaded hijab hair. You quell your conscious by telling yourself you really do need the sleep. You carefully spend a half hour combing and then drying your hair. You still have a while until bedtime, so you pray extra prayers alone. Your concentration is actually much better in this quiet in your room, without Sarah's anxious fidgeting and the lingering entertainment of her salacious gossip. You read two pages of the Quran as you do so, and then fall asleep in the middle of your "before sleep" supplications.

And then you're standing in the middle of a field. You look down to see your bare feet crinkling in the grass below. You look up into the beautiful, cloudless sky and catch your breath at the awe of the floral meadow before you. You close your eyes. You feel a gentle, warm breeze caress your cheek, and then open them, ready to run, run, run around in joy in that perfect little meadow with its perfect rainbow of flowers, and you look down to ready your legs, so light and strong they almost feel like a doe's, and you crinkle those toes once more, but then the clouds behind you shift and seem to swirl. You glance swiftly behind you to see a wall of a cloud forming to your rear. You look down at the grass, and just behind the heels of your bare feet, the grass is turning black. You turn back toward that beautiful perfect meadow with flowers so aromatic you can taste them on your tongue, and you run. You run fast, faster, fastest toward that meadow. You look back once to find that black grass so close it's almost grasping your feet, and you keep running, never looking back ... you can still see that meadow ... and to your right side, you feel an insistent nudge. You wake up instantly, look to your right. Your left, your heart still pounding, your breath whispering out in short gasps. There's nothing there. Nothing but the fear your heart retains from that dream. You sit up abruptly, feeling an overwhelming, powerful sense of having missed something. You just sit there for a while, thinking of that meadow ... that grass.

You don't sleep. You pray. You speak to Allah. You read some Quran, a little sad that it's already day 24 and you've only managed to read 5 chapters. You promise yourself that you'll do better next year, and you marathon through 10 whole pages. It takes you an hour. You blink groggily at your window, see the dawn's morning light peering shyly through your light gray curtains, and the clock firmly states that yes, it is now time for class. You get dressed. Kiss Mama on the cheek as you pass where she sits in her customary spot on the couch reading her morning Quran, her trusty beads laying ready by her side. She looks up at you and cups your cheek fondly as she finishes a verse. You squeeze her hand back and head out the door, some wistful, nostalgic feeling making you want to go back and lay your head in her lap as she plays with your hair until you fall back to sleep.

But you don't have time for that. You have classes that you need to pass for your premed degree so you can get into med school and realize your dream of becoming a doctor. You step on the gas in determination, using your left hand to steer, and your right to silence your phone.

You make dinner alone that night. Mama isn't feeling well, so you throw the soup ingredients into the pressure cooker and some boxed appetizers into the air fryer and quell Khalid and Baba's complaining as you all break your fasts together, saying that a future doctor like yourself doesn't have time to cook intricate meals. Khalid scowls broodily again, and the expression on his face hits you straight in the heart. It's the look of someone struggling. Baba laughs, not seeing or noticing Khalid's look, and says he hopes your future husband likes Friday's frozen boxed mozzarella sticks. He laughs at his own joke alone. You can't get Khalid's expression out of your head.

After breaking fast, Baba asks you if you'll go to the masjid. You say you will, and you head to Khalid's room to invite him along.

"Alright," he says, with a notable lack of enthusiasm, for him.

"Are you okay?" you ask. He stares

YOU HUG HIM AS HARD AS YOU CAN, IMAGINING THAT YOU'RE A SNAKE, AND YOU WAIT AND WAIT UNTIL YOU FEEL THE TENSENESS IN HIS SHOULDERS EASE, AND HE LEANS INTO YOUR HUG AND ABSORBS YOUR LOVE.

out the window for a few minutes before responding.

"I'm just... not having the best time at school," he finally says.

"What's going on?" you ask, fiercely trying to keep the alarm out of your voice. "What can we do?"

"Nothing!" he almost shouts. "Don't do anything, or say anything." You stare at him for a few seconds, and then you reach out and do the only thing you can think of to do—you hug him hard. You hug him as hard as you can, imagining that you're a snake, and you wait and wait until you feel the tenseness in his shoulders ease, and he leans into your hug and absorbs your love.

"We're here for you," you whisper. You let him go when you feel him pull away, and pretend not to notice when he wipes away a tear. You leave his room, pausing in front of his closed door in concern. You quickly decide, and dash out a quick note to your mom so you don't forget to remind her to give him some special attention. Before he joins you at the front door, you stretch your hands out in front of your face and utter this quick plea, "Oh Allah, please help Khalid, please grant him relief from whatever he's suffering, and guide him always. Ameen." You wipe your face as he saunters up next to you.

"AM I GOING TO MAKE IT?"
YOU ASK YOURSELF.
"NO?"
No.
YOU JUST HOPE
YOU'VE DONE ENOUGH.

"You and Mama are so paranoid about the evil eye," he scoffs. You pretend to smile. You see Baba has not waited, and dig for your keys in your purse to unlock the door to your own car. You buckle your seatbelt, and look into your mirror to fix your hijab, noticing you've forgotten to put on foundation but actually happy to be heading to the masjid free of adornment. You wait until Khalid buckles up, and then back out of the driveway.

This time you play Quran on low volume in the background. Khalid doesn't protest. The verse about Ramadan from Surah Al-Baqarah is recited, and it takes you back to the days of your childhood. The time Khalid came home from school spitting, and you laughing when he explained that he thought fasting meant you couldn't swallow your own saliva. Decorating the house with homemade stars and moons and dollar store streamers with Mama. Winding decorative lights around the bannister with a laughing three-year-old Khalid by your side. Racing outside with him when he was seven to check if the crescent was visible yet, so excited you both forgot to put on shoes and ran back inside with reddened, chapped feet.

Your phone chimes a text. You roll your eyes with a smile as you anticipate a text from Sarah. You look down and reach your hand across the gear shifter to attempt to switch your phone onto silent mode one-handed, never noticing the black pickup truck barreling your way.

The impact of the truck with your car explodes the airbags. You feel a piece of plastic slam into your chest, so hard it feels like a swipe from a sword. You try to breathe, but you can't. You gasp for breath, but your lungs don't seem to want to work. You look over at Khalid, unconscious but unharmed.

You try and try and try to breathe as you stare, stare at your beloved brother. The air won't come. You try and try until you begin to feel nothing.

Am I going to make it? you ask yourself.

No?

No.

You just hope you've done enough.

You feel an insistent nudging at your right side. Wake up, Mama says. Wake up for suhoor. You slowly, almost miraculously, awaken to another Ramadan day.

HANNAH MATUS, Esq. is a licensed attorney in Ohio. She is the author of *A Second Look*, a novel selected as The Best Muslim Readers Choice of 2022.

A RAMADAN JOURNEY

by Martha Trunk

JOURNALING, POTATO CHIPS, AND KINDNESS

On a recent trip to London, I stopped into Foyles, one of my favorite bookstores in the world. Located on Charing Cross Road, the legendary London street of bookshops, Foyles is five floors of titles, offering a dazzling array of volumes on every topic imaginable. As I strolled amongst the stacks, a book on a shelf across the room caught my eye. Its cover was embellished with a gold and turquoise tile pattern, resembling the celestial blue dome of the Karatay Medrese in Konya, Turkey, the city of the Mevlevi dervishes. I walked over and saw that it was a notebook, and, for someone who collects notebooks, this was an appealing find. Yet it was the title on the cover that attracted me even more: *Ramadan Journal: A Daily Planner.* What could this be, I thought? It turns out that this shiny notebook was a guidebook of sorts for Ramadan. I had never seen a journal like this and was immediately curious.

Ah, Ramadan.... This month is sacred to Muslims, for it is believed that during this time, the angel Gabriel revealed the first verses of the Qur'an to the Prophet Muhammad on a night known as the "Night of Power."

I have "done" Ramadan for about 7 years now; meaning, I have fasted through the month. I originally fasted three times in Turkey, when the month corresponded with a trip there. Muslims follow the 354-day lunar calendar; this is why the month moves forward each year and the start and end dates vary. I found the experience so rewarding that I have continued to observe it in the US.

What may seem odd about this that I am not a Muslim but a Christian. And yet, I participate in this month with great joy, along with millions of Muslims. Perhaps that may seem a bit hypocritical:

how can I dip into this religion and cherry-pick just one of its most glorious manifestations, you ask? Am I but a voyeur to this faith, looking down from above like an Orientalist of old?

In a similar fashion, I have many Jewish friends who "celebrate" Christmas, and I always find this secular religious surfing amusing and a bit curious. Yet Ramadan is different—it is not a question of enjoying sparkling lights, decorated shop windows, eggnog, sugar cookies, concerts, and Christmas trees. Ramadan is tough and not for the weak of heart. It is not easy to fast from sunrise to sunset, and to go without water, as well, especially during the hot summer months.

What was inside this journal that caught my eye? The journal provided handy tips for planning this month-long spiritual journey, as well as guided questions and road maps for how to reach your destination. Meal planners, shopping lists, Qur'an readings, and prayer trackers are included—and all quite helpful. Having a journal to document the month of Ramadan may seem like an efficiently modern take on an ancient tradition, but "when in doubt, jot it out!" is one of my mottos, so I appreciated this guided approach to maximizing the rewards of the month. But most of all, reading the passages in this journal allowed me to reconfirm

the spiritual reasons why I participate in this ritual. As I flipped through the pages of the Ramadan Journal, I noted many of the thoughts that go through my mind when my stomach starts growling and my head gets dizzy, and why I seemingly masochistically persist in doing something this hard.

Ramadan is more than just fasting and a growling stomach. Ramadan is a time of physical discipline, yes, but it is also a spiritual one. It offers an opportunity to engage in a deep contemplation of one's relationship with God, but also with yourself and your fellow human beings. It makes you feel a part of something that is much bigger than your daily existence, and its rewards for me come from many levels.

On a primary level, the physical challenge is hard (that is an understatement), but it is also rewarding, because it helps to recall the frailty of life. It confirms to me that I am strong; stronger than I ever thought possible, and that my will is much tougher than any tempting bag of potato chips. It teaches the potential of your maximum, not your minimum, and I am given the time and space to discover that of which I am capable. Ramadan clarifies—much like Covid did for me—what you can do without and what you truly need to be happy. It helps you to let go of consumerism on many levels, to say no to futile things; all im-

> "WHEN THE MONTH OF RAMADAN STARTS, THE GATES OF HEAVEN ARE OPENED AND THE GATES OF HELL ARE CLOSED AND THE DEVILS ARE CHAINED."
>
> PROPHET MUHAMMAD
> PEACE BE UPON HIM

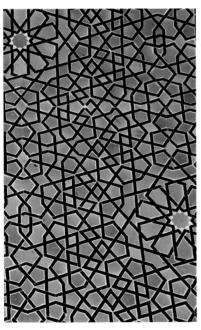

Karatay Madrasa, Konya, Turkey

portant considerations in our modern world full of goals of social, health, and climate sustainability. Oddly enough, the month of fasting reinvigorates the body, and at the end of the month, you feel pure and as triumphantly robust as if you had completed a marathon—and to boot, you may drop a few pesky pounds along the way!

On a second level, Ramadan gives an opportunity to pull back from the ruckus of daily life and reflect on many things. Things forcibly slow down, and you move and speak more deliberately, and think a bit more deeply. There is no idle chit chat when your mouth is bone dry, that is certain! This is the part of Ramadan that I savor the most, because no matter what your beliefs (or non-beliefs), you can focus on being positive and improving your life. You can access the nagging questions of your existence and try to find a way to answer them. The Prophet Muhammad said, *"When the month of Ramadan starts, the gates of heaven are opened and the gates of hell are closed and the devils are chained."*

Who/what are those devils he refers to? Well, after a month of fasting, you will have identified a few of those devils in your life—those ugly parts of you that are not in balance, be they overinflated egos, a weakness for alcohol and drugs, bad relationships, selfishness, money, or addictions to potato chips. They will arise their heads and manifest themselves clearly. Ramadan gives the opportunity to consider your bad physical and mental habits, and how to amend them to practice better ones, much like the famous New Year's resolutions. You see more clearly a path towards moderation, consideration, and harmony.

Ramadan also gives you the opening to go beyond your little (or for some people, big) ego and to think of others. Charity is an important part of Ramadan, which is a time for Muslims to reach out to people in need. Helping people and sharing food is theologically central to Islam, with each Muslim called to tithe 2.5% of his earnings to charity. This tithing is generally done during the last part of this holy month, when giving is considered especially holy. Ramadan as such allows you to connect with your fellow human beings and reach out to the community in which you live. This month becomes a moment when you count your blessings and feel compassion for others. For example, in New York, millions of dollars are given to charity each Ramadan. An article in the New York Times from April 29, 2022, entitled "Why Ramadan Generates Millions in Charitable Giving Every Year," indicated that the 800,000 Muslims in New York donate some $610 million to charity during the month of Ramadan. Muslim households on average donate 33 percent more than non-Muslim households in the United States.

All is not parched mouths and growling stomachs during Ramadan. There is much joy and laughter, too. Perhaps Muslims focus on their connection to God and their fellow man during the day, but in the evening, it becomes a time of joyous celebration spent with friends and family. Delicious iftar meals (the meal at sundown that breaks the fast), long conversations into the night over countless glasses of tea and juice, trips to the mosque, group Qur'an readings and happy moments shared with loves ones form priceless bonds and memories. It is like celebrating Christmas morning each evening for 30 days.

AT THE END OF RAMADAN, YOU FEEL PURE
AND AS TRIUMPHANTLY ROBUST AS IF YOU HAD
COMPLETED A MARATHON.

However, as a Christian, I am perhaps missing out on one of the most important aspects of Ramadan, and that is connecting with the Qur'an through daily readings and prayer sessions. The entire Qur'an is read throughout the month, at a pace of about twenty pages a day, at special readings at the mosque (tarawih) or at home (the journal included a handy reading chart to complete the reading in 30 days). This connection to the holy text is the foundation of Ramadan, and I stand a bit aside from this, for the Qur'an is not my holy book. Yet I read passages from the Qur'an throughout the month, with the hope that I would perceive the wisdom and inspiration its message can provide on a universal level.

Similarly, since I am not a Muslim, I don't go to the mosque during Ramadan for those special nightly prayer sessions, nor do I participate in the flurry of evening iftar activities. For me, it's a bit of a solitary exercise to do Ramadan, for I usually break the daily fast all by myself, which would be inconceivable in a Muslim country. I am fine with that, because in reality I am not alone: I am joined in that exact moment of time with millions of Muslims throughout the world, and I find that instant of community exhilarating. At that moment I connect especially with my Muslim friends. When I lift the date from the plate to break fast as did the Prophet Muhammad and take that first sip of soup, I see all their faces swimming in front of me, and how happy I am to share that moment of victory with them.

An interesting experiment was done in Germany in 2018, led by a German Muslim group called Datteltäter. They asked several non-Muslim German influencers if they would like to participate in a Ramadan experiment. They were asked to do 4 things: 1) fast like a Muslim for four days; 2) take one minute, five times a day (corresponding to the Muslim daily prayers) to think about a reason to be happy, 3) make someone you don't know happy via a random act of kindness or by a concerted donation; 4) come together and share an iftar dinner with other people. The group—hesitant at first, especially concerning that challenging fasting business—signed up and later shared their experiences, trials, and rewards on YouTube, and I noted that their observations often coincided with mine.

So, in the end, is it so peculiar that a Christian would want to participate in the journey of Ramadan? Am I justified to take only the good stuff, like those Christmas trees, when one is not a full-fledged Muslim? I like to dream

that people can live in a meta-sphere where we can all be separate and come together in our beliefs every once in a while, such as at Thanksgiving or Christmas or Ramadan, and reap the rewards of a more compassionate view of the world. Can't reading the Qur'an provide me with insights and an enhanced spiritual outlook? Can't Islam teach me a different story of humanity than the one I know? Can't giving to charity remind me of the Franciscans and Jesus washing the feet of the leper? Can't engaging in that intimate conversation that is prayer bring me closer to God? Can't reflecting about my nega-

tive habits, ego, and thoughts make me a better person? Can't thinking about mercy, compassion, and gratitude connect me more closely with the world around me? Can't making charitable pledges instill me with a different sense of social awareness and consciousness?

Ramadan also recalls to me a very significant trial in the life of Jesus. After being baptized by John the Baptist, Jesus went into the desert and fasted for 40 days and nights. He was then tempted three times by Satan, but Jesus successfully refused each temptation and returned to Galilee to begin his ministry. Was not Jesus engaging in the same spiritual battle and seeking the same rewards as a Muslim does during Ramadan? I believe so, and this thought resolutely connects me as a Christian to Ramadan. As noted in the "*Inshirah*" chapter of the Qur'an ("The Opening of Heart"), after hardship comes ease.

The Ramadan Journal I saw at Foyles included pages for jotting down your personal thoughts, goals, and lessons learned from the Qur'an readings and throughout the month of reflection. No matter what your beliefs, you can "jot it out" and take time to voice what you are feeling on paper. And rereading those jottings and the emotions they evoke may well remind us that the values of Ramadan last far beyond a single month.

WAS NOT JESUS ENGAGING IN THE SAME SPIRITUAL BATTLE AND SEEKING THE SAME REWARDS AS A MUSLIM DOES DURING RAMADAN?

MARTHA TRUNK is an author, historian, and translator based in New York. She writes on art, history, and interfaith issues.

WHEN

Muslims follow a lunar calendar (Hijri). Ramadan starts when the new moon is sighted. If the moon is not sighted, then fasting starts following the thirtieth day of Sha'ban, the month that precedes Ramadan. The Prophet said: "Fast after you have seen it [the new crescent] and end the fast [at the end of the month] when you see it." Fasting becomes obligatory for all Muslims around the world after the new moon is seen anywhere in the world.

WHO

It is obligatory for every sane and healthy Muslim adult to fast. Minors, travelers, sick people, elderly, breast-feeding, menstruating women or those having post-childbirth bleeding are exempt from fasting. Parents can encourage their children to fast to get accustomed to it. Adults who cannot fast can feed a poor person daily and, if they can, later make up for the days they missed.

WHY

"O you who believe! Fasting is prescribed for you, as it was prescribed for those before you, that you may become righteous." (Qur'an 2:183).

WHAT

One must indicate his or her intention for fasting before dawn as an act of the heart. Eating pre-dawn meal (suhoor) with the intention of fasting indicates one's intention.

SCHEDULE

Fasting is from dawn to sunset: "Eat and drink until the white thread becomes distinct to you from the black thread of the dawn. Then strictly observe the fast until nightfall" (Qur'an 2:187).

EXCLUSIVE

Tarawih is a special prayer observed every night in Ramadan. One can do it invidually, too, but many prefer to go to a mosque and benefit from the blessings of collective prayer.

EXTRA

Fasting is obligatory during Ramadan, but it can be observed voluntarily at other times, too. Fasting six days in the month of Shawwal, which comes right after Ramadan, is reported to be as rewarding as if one fasted the entire year. The Prophet would also fast in the months of Sha'ban and Muharram. He would also regularly fast on Mondays and Thursdays throughout the year.

CELEBRATE

When Ramadan is over, Muslims celebrate Eid al-Fitr. As a part of the celebration, they gather at the mosque to observe Salat al-Fitr prayer, listen to the sermon, and greet one another. Eid is for three days, during which Muslims visit family, friends, and neighbors.

POWER

The most special time of the month of Ramadan is the Night of Power, or Destiny: Laylat al-Qadr. Praised in the Qur'an as "better than a thousand months," this night is believed to be the night the Prophet received the first revelations. Although the exact date is unknown, the 27th night of Ramadan is usually observed as Laylat al-Qadr.

RETREAT

I'tiqaf is a time of retreat for prayer and worship. Many Muslims do this during Ramadan and stay in mosques until dawn.

"FAST AND FASTER"
by Rabbi Burton Visotzky

The advent of Ramadan makes me think about my own Jewish fast days and calendar. This is especially true because the Muslim lunar calendar differs from the Jewish organization of our own holidays and year. Further, the fast of Ramadan differs from the various Jewish fast days.

It has been Jewish practice for almost two thousand years to fast on six days during our luni-solar calendar cycle. In the Jewish calendar, unlike the Christian calendars but like the Muslim one, Jews count each month by the moon. Lunar months average 29 $\frac{1}{2}$ days. Since there are twelve months per year, there are 354 days in a Jewish calendar-year. Of course, that means we are about eleven days shy of a solar calendar each year. Because we want Passover to be in the springtime and not have it be a moveable feast (like Ramadan), seven times during a nineteen-year cycle, we Jews add a leap-month. This keeps Passover in the Spring, the New Year in the autumn, fast days scattered across the year, and everyone rather confused unless they refer to the calendar on paper or online (e.g. www.hebcal.com). Christians have a solar calendar, Muslims a lunar calendar, and Jews have a luni-solar calendar.

There are two kinds of fast days during the Jewish year: major fasts that run from sunset until the stars come out the next day (approximately 25 hours), and lesser, day-time fasts that start at sunrise and end when the stars are visible (somewhat like the Ramadan daytime fast but only for one day). Of these lesser fasts, there are two related to individuals mentioned in the Hebrew Bible: the fast of Gedaliah (a governor of Judea who was assassinated during the 6th century BCE) and the fast of Esther (the heroine of the biblical book that bears her name). Then there are two more lesser fasts related to the destruction of Jerusalem. The First Jerusalem Temple was destroyed ca. 587/586 BCE and the Second Jerusalem Temple was destroyed in 70 CE. The two minor fasts commemorate the breach of the walls of Jerusalem that led to the fall of the city and ultimately the Temples.

Then there are the full-day, 25-hour major fasts. The first of these is the 9th of Av (a Hebrew month that comes during the summer). It commemorates the actual destruction of both the First and Second

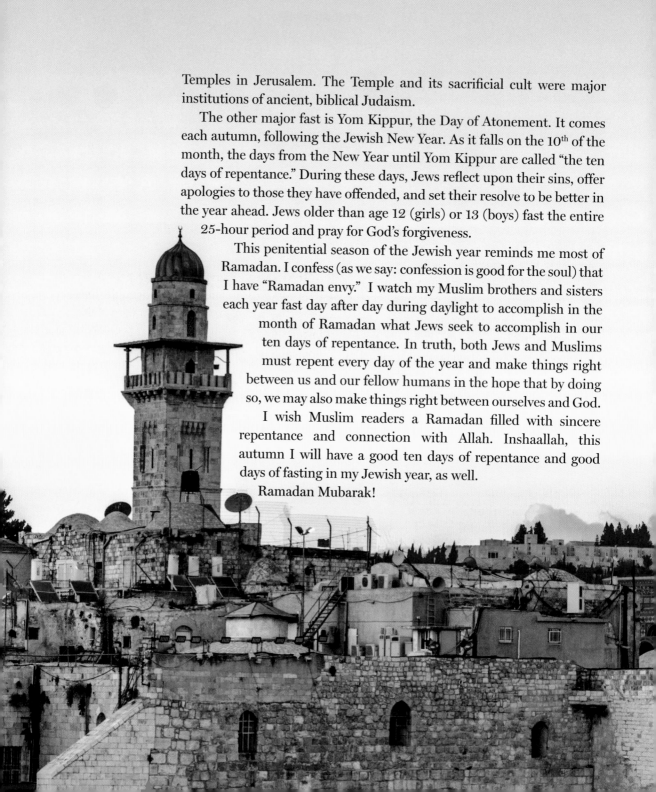

Temples in Jerusalem. The Temple and its sacrificial cult were major institutions of ancient, biblical Judaism.

The other major fast is Yom Kippur, the Day of Atonement. It comes each autumn, following the Jewish New Year. As it falls on the 10th of the month, the days from the New Year until Yom Kippur are called "the ten days of repentance." During these days, Jews reflect upon their sins, offer apologies to those they have offended, and set their resolve to be better in the year ahead. Jews older than age 12 (girls) or 13 (boys) fast the entire 25-hour period and pray for God's forgiveness.

This penitential season of the Jewish year reminds me most of Ramadan. I confess (as we say: confession is good for the soul) that I have "Ramadan envy." I watch my Muslim brothers and sisters each year fast day after day during daylight to accomplish in the month of Ramadan what Jews seek to accomplish in our ten days of repentance. In truth, both Jews and Muslims must repent every day of the year and make things right between us and our fellow humans in the hope that by doing so, we may also make things right between ourselves and God.

I wish Muslim readers a Ramadan filled with sincere repentance and connection with Allah. Inshaallah, this autumn I will have a good ten days of repentance and good days of fasting in my Jewish year, as well.

Ramadan Mubarak!

"BOTH JEWS AND MUSLIMS MUST REPENT EVERY DAY AND
MAKE THINGS RIGHT BETWEEN US AND OUR FELLOW HUMANS
IN THE HOPE THAT BY DOING SO, WE MAY ALSO MAKE THINGS
RIGHT BETWEEN OURSELVES AND GOD."

RABBI BURTON VISOTZKY, PhD, is Appleman
Professor of Midrash and Interreligious Studies
Emeritus. He is also the Director of of Milstein
Center for Interreligious Dialogue, at Jewish
Theological Seminary in New York.

LOVE THE SOJOURNER
BREAKING FAST ON THE ROAD

by Jeff Wearden

"And when you fast, do not look gloomy like the hypocrites, for they disfigure their faces that their fasting may be seen by others. Truly, I say to you, they have received their reward. But when you fast, anoint your head and wash your face, that your fasting may not be seen by others but by your Father who is in secret. And your Father who sees in secret will reward you."

the words of Jesus, recorded in Matthew 6:16-18

As a follower of Jesus, my experience of fasting has always been intensely personal, even secretive. I grew up in a Roman Catholic family, and my siblings and I attended Catholic schools. During the 40 days of Lent preceding Resurrection Sunday, my friends and I all abstained from some faavorite food or treat and obeyed the church's teaching to abstain from meat on Fridays. We were aware of Jesus' teaching about fasting, so we tried to keep quiet about the things in which we weren't indulging. As a young adult, even though I had left the Catholic church, I continued to practice fasting in obedience to the teachings of Jesus, and fasting was still a very private, personal matter.

My family and I moved to Türkiye in 2002, a few months before Ramazan started that year. We didn't really know what to expect as Ramazan approached. In the lobby of our apartment building there were always lots of colorful flyers from local supermarkets advertising all of the Ramazan favorites on sale for the big month—meat, yogurt, nuts, dried fruits, fancy desserts, and, of course, dates. It was a bit confusing. I remember my wife leafing through the flyers and thinking out loud, "So, is Ramazan a month of fasting? Or feasting?" We would later come to understand it is both.

I was teaching ESL part-time and taking Turkish lessons in the Kadıköy area of Istanbul. I took public transportation to and from work and school. Frequently, during Ramazan I would find myself on a packed bus or commuter train when the evening *ezan* sounded. Then, the most unexpected thing would occur. Total strangers, all around me, would hold their hands out in front of their chests, palms up, whisper a silent prayer, and rub their palms across their faces. Smiling, they would reach into their purse or briefcase and pull out a small plastic bag of dates which they offered to everyone around them, including me. They didn't ask whether I was a Muslim (it's obvious from looking at me that my ancestors were northern European, not Middle Eastern or Mediterranean). They didn't ask whether I had fasted that day (sometimes I had, sometimes not). Their actions seemed to communicate that they recognized our shared humanity and the challenges (like hunger) that go along with being human. Let's all just help each other on this difficult journey through life.

I remember one day in particular. It was a few years later. The war in Iraq was in full swing at the time. The war years brought some challenges, living as an American in Türkiye. Sometimes angry questions or comments would come from taxi drivers or shopkeepers. Traffic cops stopping me to check my papers. Who was I? Where was I from? What was I doing in Türkiye? I began to understand how it feels to be profiled. I never felt in danger and the situations were always pretty rapidly defused (Türks have a strong friendship reflex), but it was annoying sometimes. "Hey folks," I wanted to say, "I don't like this war any more than you do. And President Bush didn't consult with me before he started it. Don't blame me."

That day I had borrowed a friend's car to run an errand on the European side of the city. As the sun was sinking below the horizon and *iftar* was rapidly approaching, I was stuck in a long line of cars waiting to board a ferry back to the Asian side. Ahead of me was a security guard, vigorously waving for the traffic to keep moving. Just then I heard the sound of the *ezan* from the mosques all around. I was wondering what might happen, whether the ferry would be postponed. At about the same moment, the security guard lifted his eyes, made eye contact with me, the foreigner, and raised his hand for me to halt. "Great! Here it comes again," I thought to myself. "Some low-budget

TOTAL STRANGERS, ALL AROUND ME, WOULD HOLD THEIR HANDS OUT IN FRONT OF THEIR CHESTS, PALMS UP, WHISPER A SILENT PRAYER, AND RUB THEIR PALMS ACROSS THEIR FACES.

rent-a-cop with a sixth-grade education wants to throw his weight around and let off some steam about the war in Iraq and I just happen to be the nearest foreigner in sight!" The security guard approached the driver-side window with a bit of an apprehensive look on his face. I rolled down the window. He addressed me, "Sir, it's *iftar*. Can I offer you something to eat?" He held up a small plastic bag of dates. I was so guilty (I have tears in my eyes as I write this, ashamed of my arrogance and prejudice.). I had assumed the worst about him. He just wanted to be friends and help a fellow pilgrim on the journey.

Love the sojourner, therefore, for you were sojourners in the land of Egypt.
Deuteronomy 10:19

Our children were generously admitted to private Turkish schools, and my wife began teaching ESL there. Ramazan was always a busy month of iftar with classmates, friends, students, and teachers, or hosting *iftar* at our own home. We were always deeply touched by our Turkish friends' generosity and hospitality. The food was always wonderful, and we always felt so welcomed. Many times, we conversed long into the evening over bottomless cups of Turkish *çay*. Our friends were always so gracious in receiving our own clumsy ef-

THEY DIDN'T ASK WHETHER I WAS A MUSLIM. THEY DIDN'T ASK WHETHER I HAD FASTED THAT DAY. THEIR ACTIONS SEEMED TO COMMUNICATE THAT THEY RECOGNIZED OUR SHARED HUMANITY AND THE CHALLENGES THAT GO ALONG WITH BEING HUMAN.

forts at hospitality, which paled in comparison to theirs.

I felt so honored every time I was invited to *sahur*, many times at fancy restaurants and at least once at a little roadside sandwich cart because of a misunderstanding about transportation. It didn't matter whether we were seated in luxury or on a plastic stool on the sidewalk, we were happy to be together, to do life together. Our friends always communicated that they felt honored that we were a part of their community. Their inclusion of us was heartwarming and humbling at the same time. They embodied the poem attributed to Mevlana Rumi:

Come again, please, come again,
Whoever you are.

Religious, infidel, heretic or pagan.
Even if you promised a hundred times
And a hundred times you broke your
promise,
This door is not the door
Of hopelessness and frustration.
This door is open for everybody.
Come, come as you are.

Because of political oppression over the last several years, many friends from my community in Türkiye have been driven out of the country and scattered across the globe. I pray that in their new homes they will find local people who will treat them with all the hospitality and acceptance with which my family and I were treated in Türkiye.

JEFF WEARDEN and his family lived, worked, and learned in Türkiye for 15 years.

The tomb of Rumi
Konya, Turkey

FASTING TO FOCUS
IN AN AGE OF DISTRACTIONS
by Hakan Yesilova

Read and write: this is what I do for my living. Being paid for what many people do for pleasure sounds easy and enjoyable. I cannot say I disagree—and I feel very lucky—yet, I've always wished I had two things while doing my job more than anything: more pleasurable manuscripts and less distraction.

One "success" story of overcoming distraction was one Christian Bale told about himself during the filming of one of his cult films, *The Machinist* (2004). In the movie, he plays a man who suffers from insomnia in addition to delusions and a feeling of guilt, as a result of which he becomes emaciated. Bale delivers an outstanding performance as viewers can vividly see how deeply he has immersed himself into the role: he went on a strict diet for more than four months and lost 62 pounds. A positive outcome of this "fasting" was not how he looked with his protruding bones, but how he could focus: "... somehow, losing all the physical weight put all the energy into my brain. I only slept two hours a night and all I wanted to do was read. I would just sit and read endlessly, and I found that I could read without stopping and needing to move and get a distraction. I could just sit and read for 10 hours straight without moving a muscle" [1]. How I wish I could do that: focus and read for hours and hours—though of course without emaciation!

THE REAL INTENTION BEHIND FASTING AND ITS MANY PRACTICAL—AND HEALTHY—IMPACTS CAN OPEN A WINDOW ON HOW TO LIVE A PURPOSEFUL LIFE AND REALIZE OUR FULL POTENTIAL—A LIFE WHERE WE'RE CONSTANTLY MINDFUL AND LIVE EVERY MOMENT TO THE FULLEST.

Distraction

Distraction has been a part of the human story from the very beginning. According to the scriptures, Satan did all he could to distract Adam and Eve from their peaceful life in the Garden of Eden; he did all he could to distract Abraham and his son on their greatest march of self-mastery; he did all he could to distract Jesus with all possible temptations.

We usually explain our accomplishments and failures by how much we focus or how much we are distracted. Recently, this has become a serious matter, especially after the devastating impacts of the Covid pandemic on students' learning. Many people, especially younger generations, are going through what is called "distracti-pression," [2] unable to focus while fighting with anxiety. In 2021, a total of 337,054,544 prescriptions were written for antidepressants in the United States. This number was 313,665,918 in 2017. Across the same time period (2017-2021), teenagers showed a 41 percent increase in antidepressant use, corresponding to around 19 million people [3]. Distraction combined with other psychological problems is likely to take huge tolls in our education system and workforce, the implications of which will be seen soon. Another thing that Covid has exacerbated, is that many of us also feel like we're "drowning in work"; we are unable to focus in front of our computers for we keep "cycling through open tabs" every few minutes and are frequently distracted by "email, instant messaging, remote-meeting apps, work-flow and project management software" that were meant to be digital tools to help us work better "with more focus and efficiency" [4].

"Focus" to make sense of life

Focusing vs. distraction is as relevant to our daily rou-

"... LOSING ALL THE PHYSICAL WEIGHT PUT ALL THE ENERGY INTO MY BRAIN. I ONLY SLEPT TWO HOURS A NIGHT AND ALL I WANTED TO DO WAS READ. I FOUND THAT I COULD READ WITHOUT STOPPING AND NEEDING TO MOVE AND GET A DISTRACTION."

Christian Bale commenting on his experience of fasting to get ready for his character in The Machinist.

tines at home, work, or school, as it is to how we project a vision for our lives, how we perceive the world, and make sense of it. Many of us make plans for college, our career, summer vacations, marriage, etc., while many drift wherever the winds of external events carry us. Assuming that we have committed ourselves to the plans and accomplished our goals for a good education and successful career, how much of these accomplishments help us understand who we are, and how relevant are they to our innate potential? Is being human something we define according to our college diploma or profession?

We need to "focus" more to appreciate our position in this world as the most honorable creation equipped with unique qualities like willpower and spirit; a creation who is not just any accidental combination of biological forms and star dust. Fasting, for that matter, is an important tool that can help us free ourselves from the attachment to our material being, bodily desires, and many distractions resulting from them, by way of a serious action: cutting off their lifeline. Especially in wealthy nations where we are blessed with all kinds of tastes—many of which not so healthy—if we cannot curb ourselves, we tend to run from one craving to another, never fully satisfied. Fasting might be difficult in the beginning, but as we learn to tame our cravings and be independent of addictions even to things as basic as tea or coffee, we can reach a level of brain power and attention as Christian Bale did while preparing for *The Machinist*. This is one of the wisdoms why many religious traditions prescribe fasting in one form or another: to unleash the real human potential that is often suppressed under distractive habits and lifestyles.

Fasting Ramadan is one strong pillar of Islamic faith. Though, we should not forget that Ramadan is not only about staying away from food from dawn to sunset, nor is it something Muslims only do for good health or for more brain power. "Whoever does not leave bad words and behavior while fasting, God does not need him to leave food and drink," Prophet Muhammad, peace be upon him, reportedly said [5]. In another tradition, he said, "I have been sent to perfect the good character" [6]. One fasting without these objectives in mind "gets nothing but hunger," [7] the Prophet also emphasized.

Fasting is not the only solution to all the problems of the world. But the real intention behind fasting and its many practical—and healthy—impacts can open a window on how to live a purposeful life and realize our full potential—a life where we're constantly mindful and live every moment to the fullest. It is not a coincidence that, according to the scriptures, Jesus became who he was meant to be when he resisted Satan's temptations when he was fasting.

Notes
1. Christian Bale Breaks Down His Most Iconic Characters | GQ
2. https://www.nytimes.com/2022/07/09/style/medication-depression-anxiety-adhd.html
3. Ibid.
4. https://www.nytimes.com/interactive/2023/01/23/magazine/cal-newport-interview.html?searchResultPosition=1
5. Al-Bukhari 1903.
6. Al-Muwatta' 1614.
7. Ibn Maja 1690.

HAKAN YESILOVA is the editor of *The Fountain* a bimonthly magazine on life, knowledge, and belief.

O YOU WHO BELIEVE! FASTING IS PRESCRIBED FOR YOU, AS IT WAS PRESCRIBED FOR THOSE BEFORE YOU, THAT YOU MAY BECOME RIGHTEOUS.

QUR'AN 2:183

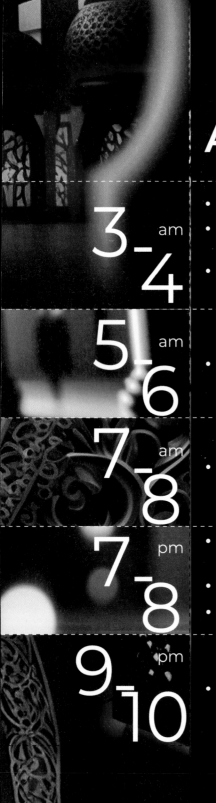

A DAY IN RAMADAN

3–4 am

- *Wake up before dawn for suhoor – the early breakfast*
- *Wash for ablutions to stand for prayers (tahajjud), read the Qur'an, say dhikr.*
- *Take your last bits of food and drinks (better not go to extremes!)*

5–6 am

- *Morning prayer (fajr)*

7–8 am

- *Head to school, work, or, if you don't have to, take a nap!*

7–8 pm

- *Break the fast (iftar dinner) (better if start with a date or water)*
- *Evening prayer (maghrib)*
- *Tea time!*

9–10 pm

- *Tarawih prayer (better at the mosque)*